Paintings by Arthur T. Lee, 1848, depict Indians watching
an Army train (above) and West Texas near Fort Davis (below)

Cornerstones of Freedom

The Story of

THE LONE STAR REPUBLIC

By R. Conrad Stein

CHILDRENS PRESS ®

CHICAGO

In 1835, the village of San Antonio was the capital and most important city in Texas.

Library of Congress Cataloging-in-Publication Data

Stein, R. Conrad.
  The story of the Lone Star Republic.

  (Cornerstones of freedom)
  Summary: Follows the history of Texas from the
first settlements of Americans on Spanish land in
the 1820s to its annexation as an official state
in 1845.
  1. Texas—History—Juvenile literature. [1. Texas
—History—To 1846] I. Title. II. Title: Lone Star
republic. III. Series.
F386.3.S74 1988   976.4   87-35467
ISBN 0-516-04735-3

Childrens Press®, Chicago
Copyright ©1988 by Regensteiner Publishing Enterprises, Inc.
All rights reserved. Printed in the United States of America.

Never had Moses Austin seen so inviting a country as Texas. The soil seemed to beg for farmers. Austin rode through streams that ran diamond clear. He looked with awe upon the prairie grasses that towered high over his head. Yet, in 1820 when Austin made his journey, this amazingly fertile land was almost untouched by settlers. Spain had claimed Texas almost 3 centuries earlier, but fewer than four thousand Spanish citizens tilled its soil.

In San Antonio, the capital city of Texas, Moses Austin discussed his plan with the Spanish governor. He wished to bring three hundred American farm families to Texas. The governor hesitated. He knew Americans to be land-hungry people who constantly sought to expand their borders. But if the American farmers agreed to become Spanish subjects, they would certainly help to develop Texas. After confer-

Street scene in San Antonio

Moses Austin (right) and his son Stephen (far right)

ring with his superiors, the Spanish governor agreed to give Austin the land he needed to start his farming community.

Moses Austin died shortly after returning to his Missouri home. So the task of establishing an American colony in Texas fell to his son Stephen. Stephen Austin was a frail, bookish man who enjoyed playing the flute. He preferred to live in a city rather than on a raw frontier farm. Nevertheless, Stephen spent the rest of his life fulfilling his father's dream. Today Stephen Austin is called the "Father of Texas."

In 1821 Austin's followers broke soil on a well-watered plain along the Brazos River. The pages of Texas history refer to those pioneer Texas families as the Old Three Hundred. Word soon reached the colony that far to the south Mexican patriots had overthrown their Spanish overlords and founded the new nation of Mexico. At first this political revolution did little to disturb the lives of Texas farmers.

Thanks to hard work and tremendous sacrifices, the American community in Texas thrived. The settlers grew corn, vegetables, and cotton. All was not perfect, however. Men enjoyed long hunting trips, while women were left with backbreaking, never-ending chores, such as weeding the garden, washing clothes, and cooking. Of those early days one woman said, "Texas was heaven for men and dogs, but hell for women and oxen."

News of the fertile land in Texas traveled east, and what was called Texas Fever swept the United States. Hundreds of Americans living on the log-cabin frontier boarded up their houses, scrawled the letters GTT (Gone to Texas) on the door, and headed west. By 1830 Americans in Texas outnumbered the old Spanish settlers four to one.

As the years of American settlement progressed,

Painting by Carl G. Von Iwonski portrays the log cabins built by Austin's settlers.

hostility grew between the American Texans and the Mexican government. The Texans demanded home rule privileges, such as the power to set up courts in their own villages. The Mexicans, on the other hand, fumed over the fact that Texans often ignored Mexican law. Most of the American Texans were from southern states, and many brought slaves with them to Texas. The practice of slavery was strictly against Mexican law. Stephen Austin, a patient diplomat, tried to moderate the arguments that broke out between American colonists and Mexican government leaders, but most of his efforts were in vain.

Slaves were used to pick Texas cotton.

Sam Houston inspired
courage in his men.

In 1830 the Mexican government, afraid of being
overwhelmed by Americans, banned further
immigration to Texas. However, Mexico lacked
sufficient soldiers to police Texas's long borders, and
Americans continued to pour into the province. One
American, who entered Texas in 1832, soon thun-
dered into the pages of history. He was Sam
Houston.

Houston was thirty-nine years old when he rode
into Texas. Already he had been a war hero, the
governor of Tennessee, and an often mentioned can-
didate for president of the United States. But a

shattered marriage broke his spirit and put a temporary halt to his political career. Despondent, he drifted toward Texas. While on the trail Houston saw what he believed to be a message from God. He later wrote, "An eagle swooped down near my head, and then, soaring aloft with the wildest screams, was lost in the rays of the setting sun. I knew that a great destiny waited for me in the West."

In his new home Houston joined sides with the Texans whose tempers raged against the government of Mexico. The fatal blow came when a cunning army general named Antonio López de Santa Anna became Mexico's dictator. When Santa Anna seized power, even the mild-mannered Stephen Austin urged, "War is our only recourse. No halfway measures, but war in full." Gunfire between the two

The Alamo was established about 1718 as a Catholic mission.

sides erupted in October 1835, at the town of Gonzales. Three weeks later a small force of Texans drove a Mexican army unit out of San Antonio. The last skirmish of that battle was fought in a crumbling, century-old mission church called the Alamo.

The Texan and the Mexican forces each believed that God marched on their side. The Mexicans regarded Texans as a slave-owning ungrateful people who dared to rebel against the mother country that had given them millions of acres of free land. The Texans believed they were bringing the golden gift of American civilization to a nation ruled by a vicious dictator. Many hundreds of Mexicans, who had lived in Texas for generations, joined forces with the Americans to fight against Santa Anna. History teaches that religious wars are the cruelest of all conflicts, and the war that rocked Texas was fought with religious zeal.

From the east, hoards of eager young men journeyed to Texas to join the American ranks. Some of the volunteers were already larger-than-life heroes. Davy Crockett, who grew up on the Tennessee frontier, came. His friends claimed Davy could shoot the wick off a candle at three hundred feet. Jim Bowie, the developer of a deadly knife, came. As a youth in Louisiana, Bowie enjoyed riding on the backs of alligators and stalking deer with a lasso. William

Only four people survived the ninety-minute attack on the Alamo: an officer's wife, her baby and her Mexican nurse, and a young black boy.

Travis, an idealistic lawyer from Alabama, came. His courage became legendary. Travis, Crockett, Bowie, and a force totaling about two hundred men gathered at the Alamo and converted the church grounds into a fort. In March 1836, a battle there marked the bloody beginnings of a new nation.

Amid the cracking of rifles and the booming of cannons, four thousand Mexican soldiers stormed the Alamo's walls. Commanding the Mexican troops was none other than the hated dictator, Antonio López de Santa Anna. General Santa Anna flew a blood-red flag while his army band played the grim *Deguello*—"The Fire and Death Song." Every Alamo defender knew the flag and the music meant that Santa Anna intended to take no prisoners.

The battle lasted ninety terrifying minutes. One Mexican officer wrote, "The Texans defended desperately every inch of the fort." But outnumbered twenty to one, the men of the Alamo had no chance. Most Texans died at their posts. The few who surrendered or tried to hide were rounded up and executed by Santa Anna. As a further insult Santa Anna ordered the bodies of the Texans burned, denying them a proper burial.

While gunshots still rang at the Alamo, Houston and some Texans met at the tiny town of Washington-on-the-Brazos about 150 miles from

San Antonio. There, on March 2, 1836, they signed the Texas Declaration of Independence. It ended with the words, "We do hereby resolve and declare that our political connection with the Mexican nation has forever ended; and that the people of Texas do now constitute a free and independent republic."

Officially the nation that emerged after this declaration was called the Republic of Texas. A republic is a country that has no king or queen. Writers called independent Texas the Lone Star Republic after the solitary star on its flag. The name stuck, and Texas is now called the Lone Star State.

Few nations ever came into being under greater peril than did Texas. At the moment its leaders were signing the Declaration of Independence, Santa

Anna was attacking the Alamo. Just days after the Alamo's fall, Santa Anna's men defeated and slaughtered an even larger force of Texans at the town of Goliad. The twin disasters meant the Mexican army was free to rampage through Texas. Blocking the Mexican onslaught were Sam Houston and a collection of poorly armed, ill-trained frontiersmen who called themselves the Army of Texas.

Houston faced dangers from both the crafty Santa Anna and the fury building up among his own men. The Texans he commanded were enraged over the massacres at the Alamo and at Goliad, and they spoiled for a fight. But Houston, an experienced military commander, knew his rag-tag army would

A committee, under the leadership of Richard Ellis (opposite page), drafted the Texas Declaration of Independence (right). The 1893 photograph (above) shows the remains of Independence Hall at Washington-on-the-Brazos where the committee met.

stand little chance against Santa Anna's disciplined regular troops. So Houston bought time by retreating. As he retreated, Houston was forced to listen to the grumbling of his soldiers and the whispered remarks that their commander was a coward.

Dodging and falling back, Sam Houston skillfully avoided battle. When time permitted, he drilled his troops, molding the raw recruits into a tough army. Meanwhile Houston's scouts lurked on mountaintops and reported the comings and goings of Santa Anna's troops. On April 21, 1836, at the banks of the San Jacinto River, Houston gathered his men. It was time to fight.

In the morning gloom eight hundred Texans

charged into Santa Anna's camp. Though they were woefully outnumbered, the Texans fought with reckless fury. "Remember the Alamo! Remember the Alamo!" they shouted as they rushed the Mexican soldiers. In the words of one Texan the battle was "the most awful slaughter I ever saw."

The blood-crazed Texans, acting as the Mexicans had at the Alamo, mercilessly shot enemy soldiers who were willing to surrender. But almost a full day after the Battle of San Jacinto, the Texans brought to Sam Houston one very important prisoner—General Santa Anna.

Houston, who was in agony from a ghastly ankle wound, ordered Santa Anna to write a note to all the

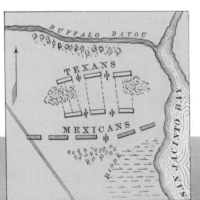

The Battle of San Jacinto by L. M. D. Guillaume. The map (left) shows how the battle lines were drawn.

Houston, recovering from a foot wound, dictates his terms of surrender to Santa Anna.

commanders of his units in Texas. Santa Anna, fearing for his life, wrote precisely what he was told to write. The note said, "I have agreed with General Houston upon an armistice, which will put an end to the war forever." Houston's scouts delivered the note, and the many thousands of Mexican troops in Texas packed their gear and marched back to Mexico. To prevent Santa Anna from regrouping and making another assault, Houston kept the Mexican general under guard for six months. The Lone Star Republic was saved. It seemed a miracle.

But the war left Texas in shambles. As a settler named William B. Dewees wrote, "The country has been completely ravaged by the armies. Houses have been robbed, provisions taken, cattle have been driven out, and the game frightened off. We have suffered exceedingly."

Even though dangers lurked everywhere, the Republic of Texas held its first election on September 5, 1836. By a landslide majority, voters selected Sam Houston to be their president. Houston chose Stephen Austin as his secretary of state. Tragically, Austin never saw the republic progress beyond the war. He died of a fever just three months after the election. "The Father of Texas is no more," Sam Houston announced. "The first pioneer of the wilderness has departed."

Houston's first order of business was to establish friendly relations with the United States. But President Andrew Jackson was reluctant to send an American ambassador to Texas. Such a move would infuriate the government of Mexico, and Jackson did not want a war with Mexico. So, without help from the United States, the infant Republic of Texas had to fend for itself.

Texas had no gold in its treasury, but its government did hold vast tracts of land. To attract new settlers the government gave the land away free for the asking. At first, each incoming family received 1,280 acres—an incredible two square miles of land. Such generous land grants spurred a great rush of immigrant farmers. The population zoomed from 35,000 settlers in 1836 to 140,000 ten years later.

Cotton and cattle were the primary enterprises in

the Lone Star Republic. Fertile land along the rivers produced an amazing two thousand pounds of cotton per acre. Even today Texas is the leading cotton-producing state in the nation. The cattle industry began when ranchers bred their animals with the Texas longhorns introduced many years earlier by Spanish ranchers. One Texan, James Taylor White, arrived from Louisiana in 1828 with just three cows. A dozen years later White owned thirty thousand head of cattle and more than forty thousand acres of ranch land.

Although Texas was primarily a farming country, several new cities developed. The bare prairie of Austin was selected to be the republic's capital, and

Austin, Texas in 1840

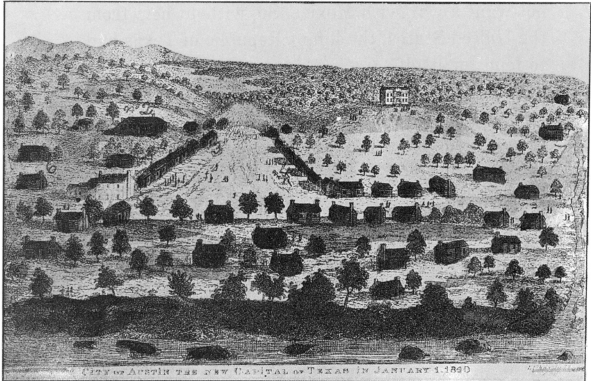

CITY OF AUSTIN THE NEW CAPITAL OF TEXAS IN JANUARY 1.1840

The wharf in Galveston

buildings began to rise there in 1839. Houston, which served as the capital from 1837 to 1839, became a leading city. Galveston was a busy port that sent Texas cotton to customers around the world.

Farmers and ranchers toiled long dusty hours on their land, but Texans also threw rollicking parties. Two fun-filled festivals were Texas Independence Day (March 2) and San Jacinto Day (April 21). Marriages, birthdays, anniversaries, or a dozen other occasions were good excuses for people to gather and celebrate. Parties often began with a thundering horse race and ended with dances that lasted until dawn. Old-time Texas dances featured high-stepping, stomping, and joyous "hootin' and hollerin'." Always there was plenty of meat to eat, since beef cost as little as bread.

Comanche Indians (bottom left) fiercely resisted intruders on their land. Cherokees (bottom right) befriended newcomers. Many even adopted their style of dress.

Even while partying, however, frontier Texans had to be alert for Indian raids. Clashes with the Comanche tribe began during Stephen Austin's time and raged for decades. A witness described a typical Comanche attack: "The father, mother, and a son of about 14 years composed the force that had to stand up against [a Comanche band]. Through [log cabin windows] they fired out upon them. Charging the little cabin the Indians tried to break down the doors, but [the father] sprang on the table . . . and shot down, killing the lead warrior instantly. While he was reloading his gun, the boy leaped to the table and shot down a second warrior. The Indians soon gave up the fight."

Unlike the Comanches, the Cherokees of east Texas made efforts to live in peace with the settlers. The Cherokees were a favorite people of Sam Houston. As a teenager Houston once lived among the Cherokees when their nation was located in Tennessee. But under Mirabeau B. Lamar, who succeeded Houston as president, Texas forces brutally drove the Cherokees out of the republic. An elderly Cherokee chief named The Bowl died with a gleaming sword in his hand while battling the Texas militia. It was later discovered the sword had been a gift from Sam Houston.

Texas Rangers

The country's most famous peace-keeping force was the Texas Rangers. Formed originally by Stephen Austin, the Rangers were a part-time, volunteer army. Superb riders and marksmen, they fought Indians, helped keep the Mexican army at bay, and ran down cattle thieves. Adopting Indian techniques, the Rangers lived off the land and were able to track a lawbreaker for one hundred miles or more. One Texan summed up the skills of the Rangers by claiming, "The Texas Rangers can ride like a Mexican, trail like an Indian, and fight like the very devil."

For nine years, from 1836 to 1845, the Republic of Texas existed as an independent nation. From its beginnings the overwhelming majority of the republic's citizens hoped their nation would someday become a state within the United States. But two issues prevented Texas from joining the Union: Washington's fear of alienating Mexico, and the explosive question of slavery.

Today people believe that slavery was an evil institution and that its practice will forever stain United States history. Before the Civil War, however, many Americans were willing to fight and die to preserve their right to own slaves. In the

Houston was the capital of Texas from 1836 to 1839.

1840s and 1850s, wrenching arguments over slavery began to tear America apart.

The United States Congress took predictable positions when debating the Texas question. Northern states refused to admit Texas into the country because slavery was practiced there. The South, on the other hand, welcomed Texas because another slave-holding state would add strength to the South's power. Due to the standoff between the North and the South, the question of accepting Texas into the Union was delayed again and again.

Whether or not to admit Texas into the Union became an explosive issue in western towns as well as in the eastern cities of New York (bottom), Boston (opposite top), and Jersey City (opposite bottom).

ANTI-TEXAS MEETING
AT FANEUIL HALL!

Friends of Freedom!

A proposition has been made, and will soon come up for consideration in the United States Senate, to annex Texas to the Union. This territory has been wrested from Mexico by violence and fraud. Such is the character of the leaders in this enterprise that the country has been aptly termed " that valley of rascals." It is large enough to make *nine* or *ten* States as large as Massachusetts. It was, under Mexico, a free territory. The freebooters have made it a slave territory. The design is to annex it, with its load of infamy and oppression, to the Union. The immediate result may be a war with Mexico—the ultimate result *will be* some 18 or 20 more slaveholders in the Senate of the United States, a still larger number in the House of Representatives, and the balance of power in the hands of the South! And if, when in a minority in Congress, slaveholders browbeat the North, demand the passage of gag laws, trample on the Right of Petition, and threaten, in defiance of the General Government, to hang every man, caught at the South, who dares to speak against their "domestic institutions,"what limits shall be set to their intolerant demands and high handed usurpations, when they are in the majority ?

All opposed to this scheme, of whatever sect or party, are invited to attend the meeting at the Old Cradle of Liberty, to-morrow, (Thursday Jan. 25,)at 10 o'clock, A. M., at which time addresses are expected from several able speakers.

Bostonians ! Friends of Freedom !! Let your voices be heard in loud remonstrance against this scheme, fraught with such ruin to yourselves and such infamy to your country.

January 24, 1838.

The above cartoon depicts President Polk welcoming Texas as a state while some congressmen are trying to stop the process. Below, Texas troops are being reviewed after Texas is admitted as a state.

Houston,
Texas, 1859

Texas finally became part of the United States
largely due to the political skill of crafty old Sam
Houston. Houston hinted to Washington politicians
that Texas would soon sign an alliance with
America's rival, Great Britain. Actually Houston's
threat was a thinly veiled lie. Texas leaders had no
real intention of teaming up with England. But just
the possibility of having a British ally on their country's western borders frightened U.S. congressmen
into opening the door to Texas.

Early in 1845 the United States Congress passed
a joint resolution to annex (or acquire) the Republic
of Texas. Texas voters later approved this annexation. On December 29, 1845, Texas became the twen-
ty-eighth American state. As was expected the

State seal of Texas

Texas coat of arms

annexation of Texas and its subsequent statehood infuriated the Mexican government. To the Mexicans Texas was still a rebellious colony, and America's action amounted to a theft of territory. The annexation of Texas was one of the major causes of the Mexican-American War, which raged from 1846 to 1848.

Despite the fear of war, bands played and crowds cheered in dozens of Texas towns when the gallant Lone Star flag was replaced with the American Stars and Stripes. For nine years the Republic of Texas had stood alone through Indian wars and the constant threat of invasion from Mexico. Now the outsider had finally become part of the family. Anson Jones, the Republic of Texas's last president, spoke for every proud Texas citizen when he said, "The Lone Star of Texas has passed on to become fixed in that glorious constellation, the American Union."

BRITISH NORTH AMERICA
TREATY LINE OF 1818

OREGON
COUNTRY
CESSION
1846

Portland

UNORGANIZED
TERRITORY

MINNESOTA
TERRITORY

Oregon Trail

WI

MI

California
Trail

Mormon Trail

IA

Sacramento

Salt Lake City

Oregon Trail

IL

Nauvoo

MEXICAN CESSION
1848

Independence

IN

Sante Fe
Trail

MO

KY

Old Spanish Trail

Santa Fe

TN

Los Angeles

AR

MS

GADSDEN
PURCHASE
1853

TEXAS ANNEXATION
1845

AL

LA

North
Pacific
Ocean

MEXICO

Gulf of Mexico

After the annexation of
Texas, settlers began
flocking to the state in
increasing numbers.
Eventually, the frontier was
pushed westward to the
Pacific coast.

Catching Wild Horses on the Prairie.

RUINS OF THE ALAMO.

PHOTO CREDITS

About the Author

R. Conrad Stein was born in Chicago and was graduated from the University of Illinois with a degree in history. He now lives in Chicago with his wife, who is also an author of books for young readers, and their daughter, Janna. Mr. Stein has written many other books, articles, and short stories for young people.

14677